Chrysalis

*A Poetic Journey through
the Spiritual Life*

Cassandra

This publication and its characters are protected by copyright. Unauthorized reproduction, distribution, or transmission in any form or by any means, including photocopying, recording, or other electronic or mechanical methods, is strictly prohibited without prior written permission from the publisher. Limited quotations in reviews and certain noncommercial uses permitted by copyright law are exempted. All rights reserved.

Paperback ISBN: 979-8-9899836-0-5
Hardcover ISBN: 979-8-9899836-1-2

©2024 Copyright Cassandra
All Rights Reserved
Printed in the United States of America

The e-book maintains the original design of the print edition, ensuring that all elements are fixed in place. Readers can easily zoom in and enlarge the content using the pinch and zoom functions while previewing in landscape mode.

Image Credits: Shutterstock
Image Credits: iStock photos
Actual photo of 'Cass O Rae'

Introduction

Chrysalis is my collection of poems I composed from the age of fifteen to forty-six. Earthbound was recorded by my band Harsh Reality in 1992 on our only demo "Down the Drain."

Cass O' Rae and Zahra are about horses I personally owned. I think the subject matter of these shows the progression of my spiritual journey, culminating in witnessing the miracles of God myself at Marmora, Canada.

I hope you enjoy reading these compositions as much as I enjoyed writing them at that inspired moment of my life. Many heartfelt thanks to my Lord and God-the Eternal Father for my talent, to Jesus Christ my Savior, to the Holy Spirit my guide, and to Mama Mary. Also, thank you to my ever-faithful husband Eric, who for years has tolerated my attention to my numerous literary projects.

God Bless each one of you!

I love you!
Cassandra

Mountain of Trash

See the trash as they pile it mountain high,
More mounds of it as the world spins by.

All our garbage goes to the dump,
To be buried into one big hump.

When will it ever stop?
When the garbage reaches the top?

We don't realize we're our own trash,
But we'll find out after the big crash.

Our whole Earth will be nothing but waste,
A piece of clear land we wish we could taste.

So why can't we make our garbage into electricity?
And make our Earth clean, fresh and pretty?

1984

Dreams Take Flight

All alone on a cold, rainy night,
Wishing my dreams could take flight.
Desperate for a spark that feels right,
Wanting to leave I set my sights.

I know someday I'll see,
Fate will smile on me.
Carry my doubts without a fee,
And let my mind go wild and free.

Shrug the cold off and start anew,
Believe in everything you want to do.
Fear in those who want not,
Are the first to be forgot.

Bursting stars lead the way,
For a new start every day.
Be strong with all of your might,
For when your dreams do take flight.

Captured star light burning bright,
Eliminate my darkened sight.
Brightened wings carry me on flight,
To be with destiny tonight.

Hope burning inside of me,
Doubts and fears are now set free.
Trade in pain for a new glory,
Live a river for the sea.

My soul is tired,
But I won't give in.
My mind keeps pushing,
Until I win.

Don't want to be left out in the cold,
Waiting for all my wishes to unfold.
I won't give in at all tonight,
The future is now worth a fight.

The past has melted inside of me,
A broken wall for some to see.
Look inside of empty me,
Locked doors without a key.

Halls that lead to nowhere,
From times of living in despair.
But when the moon strikes the hand,
I'll journey to a dreamy new land.

No ticket, no fare or needed plight,
When all my dreams finally take flight.
It doesn't matter where you've been,
Cleansed in holiness or in sin.
We all have a dreamful twin,
To push us all on to win.

Wishes in the back of your mind,
Unravel a mystery you needn't find.
So, believe in yourself and take the light,
When your dreams finally take flight.

JUNE 1990

Earthbound

Come on a timeless journey with me,
And I'll show you places of wonder to see.
I am from near and afar,
A place deep inside, a dying star.

Together we will become one,
Through the same eyes much will be done.
Some goodness, some evil done to this world,
You will see it and your blood will curl.

So, sail away on the wings of time,
Blend your freed spirit with mine.
Come hear the tales of the wind and the sea,
But only if your heart escapes with me.

I breathe in the cool, crisp air,
Soon my wings will get me there.
The yellow being burns bright today,
As the idle winds carry me their way.

Clouds full of whispers I silently glide through,
Rockets of green emerald reach for the blue.
Misty mountains that loom like gods,
White ice lay upon them like rods.

Velvet oceans cry out in vain,
Diamonds from my eyes fall like rain.
Crystal clear lakes catch my eye,
But soon will the intruder make them die?

Blackness now drapes over the land,
The white being arrives on command.
Shadows of light, infinity,
Shine down on the roaring sea.

I soar down below to a place of rest,
After my long, enduring test.
Now I tuck myself in a gem for sleep,
There my spirit settles down, next day to leap.

Too much time I do spend,
Wondering if it will end.
My wings, my heart carry me far,
To the most wonderful and hopeful star.

Frozen hearts cry out in vain,
Wondering if it will stay the same.
They plunder from life's mysteries,
With razor sharp symphonies.

The guiding light will see us through,
It's there for all, me and you.
Hear the call, the desperate sound,
For I the dove am Earthbound.

1990

QUEEN

You are the Virgin who shines so bright,
You are the one of sorrow who weeps at night.
You love us all so dearly.

You are the keeper of the heavy Hands,
You are the one who watches the lands.
You love us all so dearly.

QUEEN
My Queen
Won't you pray for me tonight?

QUEEN
My Queen
Won't you guide me to the Light?

You are the one pierced with swords,
You are the one who brings us His words.
You love us all so dearly.

You are the one who helps bring salvation.
You are the one who welcomes us in the end.
You love us all so dearly.

Queen, won't you change our hearts today?
Queen, with us please stay.
Don't give up keep pleading,
Bring souls to the One who is bleeding.

Oh Queen
Oh Queen
Lead us to your Son.

QUEEN
My Queen
Won't you pray for me tonight?

QUEEN
My Queen
Won't you guide me to the Light?

JULY 2, 1995

Bloodbath

The days go by, my sins pile up,
Like refuse before me, slowly I die.

Feeling so ashamed,
I hide my face from Your Glory,
Wondering if in Your Book
is still my name.

I need cleansing, I need release,
Mercy have on me.
I need Your forgiveness.

Yeshua, won't you bathe me in Your Blood?
And wash away my sins?
Waves of love, let me drown in the flood.
Bloodbath.

Thousands of drops you shed for us,
How many spat them back in your face?
Doesn't anyone want Your love?

Bring me the cup of the one slain,
For I know when I drink
My sins to nothingness are lain.

Bloodbath
Cleanse the soul.
Bloodbath

Make us whole.
Bloodbath
Send Your fire.
Burn our sins in the pyre.

Yeshua, won't you bathe us in Your Blood?
And wash away our sins?
Waves of love, let us drown in the flood.
Bloodbath

Yeshua drown us in Your blood.

JULY 3, 1995

Reflections

Star bearer, lifter of the sea,
Bring Your plan of redemption to me.

Mountain architect, forest green,
Such splendor this soul has never seen.

The brilliance of the moon makes a cross in the sky,
The aura of it all reflected in my eye.

Radiance of dawn breaks the spell of the night,
Bringing hope to those enchanted with plight.

The dove surrounds the heart with fountains of peace,
The symbol for mankind to be set free.

Oh, come Spirit of Holiness from above,
Enkindle our beings with Your love.

DECEMBER 22, 1995

Warning

Clouds of thunder roll away,
The Lightening One present burning my eyes.
Son of Man descending upon His glorious steed,
Bringing salvation to willing souls.

Radiance envelops the lands,
No one no longer can bear to stand.
Languages fill the air we breathe,
Professing the promised foretold words.

He is here to save you and take you home,
Come aliens of this world to your Creator.
But those who follow the enemy are vanquished,
To the furnace of fiery torture forever more.

Beg for mercy sinning one,
From your Father up above.
Cleanse yourselves with the Blood of the Lamb,
Slaughtered for your love.

Creatures of light in eternal bliss sing for you,
But satan and his horde will scream too.
Burned to hideous crisps they want you!
So, choose the realm of heavenly blue.

DECEMBER 31, 1995

The Battle Within

Internal tragedy pierces my heart,
Try every morn for a new start.
These thoughts are my hell on Earth,
Praying the mind for rebirth.

Purity lost child of my soul,
Light of Heaven is my goal.
Paths of insanity block the way,
Every minute of every day.

Guard the mind with holy shield,
To the Spirit of Power do yield.
Will these thoughts my destiny be damned?
The only chance is to be saved by the Lamb.

Calling on Saints I cannot see,
And to the One of Virginity.
Slay my mind with pure love,
Help I rely on from above.

Begone demon mind,
Another hell to find.
Just leave mine,
To the one in Eternal Time!

JANUARY 13, 1996

Our Lady Of Marmora

Our Lady of Marmora,
Please offer a prayer for me.
Take me into your Immaculate Heart,
And show me how to be free.

You've given us your words of love,
You've touched and healed our hearts.
You've shown us the way to Jesus,
From us you'll never depart.

Our Lady of Marmora,
I've seen the door to Heaven,
I've seen His glory in the sun.
I've smelled the scent of roses,
I've seen the footsteps of gold as they run.
Please offer a prayer for all.

I've seen the sun pulsate,
I've found the hearts of rock.
Under your Mantle you keep us safe,
The children of your flock.

Our Lady of Marmora,
Touch my heart so deep.
Wrap me in your mantle,
Please offer a prayer for me.

AUGUST 27, 1996

Miryam

Woman pure dove song of the Earth,
Fragrant incense rising in the new morn.
Veiled beauty radiance shining forth,
Spouse of the Holy Spirit whitest ever born.

Rose of Sharon, Lily of the Valley,
Beloved of the Creator above.
Your name resounds in our hearts- "Mary!"
Your greatest virtue is unbounding love.

Gemstone, pearl, golden Ark,
Intercessor, Mediatrix, Radiant dawn.
Guide, protector with us do embark,
As we pray to be with you, beautiful fawn.

Queen of Eternity, Bearer of The Word,
Grace filled soul do help us.
In your presence we do prefer,
When at last we meet with the dust.

JULY 26, 1998

Fallen

"Look what you've done. Why?
Now you're all cast from the sky.
My brother angels, our Father cries,
My heart to you now must die.

"We were created with such beauty,
What more could you want possibly?
To Heaven forever we would be,
To dwell in bliss eternally."

"But you had to go with your pride,
To try and turn the eventide.
Now there is nowhere you can hide,
Your heart turned to black inside."

"My children, why this fight going on?
In my Heaven I want you all to belong.
Hasatan and followers no more be us among,
For I have made Mi'ka'el the one strong!"

"Now we have these empty chairs,
From the Earth to Heaven, let there be stairs.
We will create humans, it is only fair,
And give them you Yeshua to get them there!"

AUGUST 9, 1999
MONDAY 12:00 A.M.

Stallion

He glides effortlessly over the plain,
Whipping the wind with his wild mane.
He snorts one long trumpet blast,
Upon the ledge he stands at last.

He dwells upon the scene below,
The herd of beauty moving to and fro.
His destiny to rule, to be king,
And all the adventures the role would bring.

He descends upon the frenzied band,
But they scatter in a flurry over the land.
The leader with sharp teeth bared,
Rushes to challenge this new fare.

They lock in an angry and cutting embrace,
Lashing out at each other's face.
Screams fill the coming summer night,
Waiting to see who will win this fight.

The leader with age tried his best,
But youth proved more and laid him to rest.
The old one's legacy now a memory,
The new leader squeals, the new king.

The herd then returns to graze on the plain,
The stallion begins his new reign.
With snorts and blows he prances about,
No fear in his mind or one doubt.

He is the ruler now, the proud one,
Until one day it's passed on to his son.

NOVEMBER 15, 1999 10:12 P.M.

The Mockingbird

Thank you, Abba for the Mockingbird!
In the morning he wants to greet me,
With his lovely cantor of voices,
As he towers on the tree.

His many songs of beauty,
Of all creation a flight.
He glorifies You at early dawn,
And continues through the night.

He never forgets a melody,
Each one sung in perfection.
He never exhausts his repertoire,
With his Heavenly selection.

I think you imagined the mockingbird last,
Of all your birds created.
As the crowning jewel in the stream of songs,
All birds in one, to have us delighted.

JUNE 17, 2007

Bottle Scar

Here I am alone without you,
There's nothing left that I can do.
To erase you from my mind,
What we had I'll never again find.

It's been two weeks since the crash,
You couldn't stop it, happened in a flash.
Nothing in the world could have saved you,
I'm the only one that knows the clue.

Driving in your Trans,
With a bottle in your hand.
Felt that you were on top,
That the night would never stop.

Your one obsession, one step above me,
Although you said you did love me.
Was to drink on high to no end,
My feelings for you I had to pretend.

But once you lost all control,
And didn't see the curve and wall.
Your life you spent in ten seconds flat,
No one would've ever guessed that.

A person like you would waste it so,
I guess it proves you never really know.
We had met on a warm summer day,
The sparkle in your eye said we'd may.
End up together to love and care,
You understood me and played fair.

You were the best friend I ever had,
Our times together never went bad.
The things you said were so sincere,
How I wish for one moment you were here.

Why didn't you tell me?
To me you would not even speak.
That to one problem you were not strong,
Instead, were very weak.

A passion for the bottle every day,
That wouldn't ruin our lives you'd say.
I found out too late you couldn't cope,
All I could do for you was hope.

Now as I look down upon your grave,
I think of all that you had gave.
To me that will never die,
Now all I can do for you is cry.

I tried to help you,
But you would not let me.
Said there's no problem, you are free.
I see where you are, but how?
I know and think you are free now.

UNKNOWN DATE WRITTEN
(Not from personal experience. Was to be a song lyric for my past heavy metal band).

Zahra Blossom

She trots on the waves of air,
Her tail salutes You O Lord.

She snakes her neck in attitude,
Her nicker greets me with personality.

Her gentleness is witness of Your attribute,
Her manners give glory to you O Lord.

Her memory is fascinating,
Her quivering lip makes me smile.

Her conformation is Your perfection.
Her eyes speak of kindness.

Run now in meadows of green,
With waters streaming so serene.

No more pain or fear for you,
For now your world has passed too.

JANUARY 10, 2014

Cass O'Rae

A movie at 10 years old I did see,
With a creature so magnificent in Arabian beauty.
'The Black Stallion'-a horse dark as the night,
Wild in spirit and speedy in flight.

A passion started for me that day,
Wanting to own an offspring of 'Cass Ole'.
The desire kept on throughout my life,
Through music, faith and all of life's strife.

To ride, to own a creature so great,
So blessed, the Lord did grace me that fate.
That I would one day own a piece of my past,
From my favorite stallion to be mine at last.

O Cass, a spirit shone in your eyes,
Your great ancestor lived on from the skies.
A gem, a gent you were to me,
From Cass Ole, from movie history.

You brought me joy,
just standing by your side.
Even the way you raised your lip,
when I lovingly brushed your dark hide.

Thank you for the times you let me hug you,
For when I did I hugged him too.
Your great, great grandfather Cass Ole,
Was a gift wrapped inside of you Cass O'Rae.

And thank you O great Trinity!
For the gift deemed from Eternity.

JANUARY 11, 2014

Ice

In this frozen tundra of my soul,
This burning freeze I so well know.
Kills my restless being with entice,
Once more I'm trapped in this ice.

Free me from this biting pain,
To feel the warmth of the sun again.
Can I bargain on this price?
To release me from the ice.

Searing, scratching, no relief in sight,
With inner strength I put up a fight.
Oh, fire come burn this glacial ice.

A prism of color hides your intent,
That paralyzes and then rents.
Eternal cold that's never been nice,
Engulfed in this cocoon of piercing ice.

FEBRUARY 2, 2014

Flow

You cry out from the desert of your heart,
Hoping someone will give you a spark.
Your dreams of youth are washed up on the grave,
To life and pain, you've now become a slave.

What is here for me?
What should I do?
To these watered eyes,
Give me a clue.

There is light up there,
This I do know.
Love and peace,
To my soul they will flow.

You struggle on against the grain,
Drowning in a sea of pain.
No help from the world around,
Left to stand on broken ground.

But there is light up there,
This I do know.
Love and peace,
To my soul they will flow.

MARCH 17, 2016

www.ingramcontent.com/pod-product-compliance
Lightning Source LLC
Chambersburg PA
CBHW040734060526
44119CB00087B/380/J

About The Author

Cassandra resides in North Texas with her husband, 2 cats and 2 dogs. She's a member of the Third Order Franciscans who loves to relax by reading and stargazing.

Contact: authorcassandra@protonmail.me

www.thirdorderfranciscans.com